For Hector

HUMOUR

A little guide for mind, body and spirit

KEVIN O'DONNELL

A LION BOOK

Published by
Lion Publishing plc
Sandy Lane West, Oxford, England
www.lion-publishing.co.uk
ISBN 0 7459 5025 6

First edition 2000
10 9 8 7 6 5 4 3 2 1 0

A catalogue record for this book is available
from the British Library

Typeset in 10/14 Palatino
Printed and bound in Great Britain by
Cox and Wyman Ltd, Reading

Contents

Who Put the Smile on the Mona Lisa?

When Leonardo da Vinci painted the enigmatic smile on the Mona Lisa between 1503–06, he set the speculation rumbling. What had made her smile? And who, in fact, was she? Was she the wife of a friend, Gioconda? Whatever the truth behind the painting, he was so fond of it that he took it on all his subsequent travels.

It does not matter what, exactly, produced the smile. A broader question is, 'What puts the smile on any of our faces?'

Let's have a few laughs to start with...

Neighbours from hell!

Yes?

Oh, I'm sorry to disturb you, but I'm your new neighbour.

Come in…

Oooh, I didn't plan on staying for dinner! Fred will be wondering where I've got to…

Attack of the accents

The dinner party came to an abrupt end as Clarissa came down with a deadly dose of Yorkshire:

'Eeee, by 'eck, that crème anglaise is right bloody good!'

Not to mention Reginald's outbreak of 'Brummy':

'Oi think oi'll turn in for a kip, oi will!'

'Oh, how vulgar,' chirped the hostess as she lowered her glasses and coughed with embarrassment.

The winter had seen a deadly epidemic of lower-class accents striking where one least expected it. The virus acted by reactivating the childhood dialect of its victim.

Imagine this crazy situation jumping out of a zany comedy series into reality. What if we couldn't disguise our origins, and the carefully cultivated images we sometimes like to project?

We are not amused!

Humour is like a jumping germ that strikes us down and reveals the real person inside. It is revelatory, honest and unpredictable.

What makes us laugh? Why do we do it? Is it vain and silly, or deeply and profoundly human – spiritual, even? We won't be asking Queen Victoria. We know what her answer would be!

We are not amused!

How Peculiar!

Humans and Laughter

The first laugh

We hear a good deal about the last laugh, but not the first. I can recall the moment when my eldest child first laughed – not just a smile, but a full giggle. This was a special moment!

First-laugh celebrations

The Navajo Indians celebrate a baby's first laugh with a party. The food is provided by all those who happened to be present when it occurred – or by the person who caused the laughter in the first place. It is one of the initiation rites into human life. The grandmother says a blessing prayer, and sweets and salt are handed out to betoken good fortune.

Human being

The Greek philosopher Aristotle said that we laughed sometime before our fortieth day, and then we became human. If humour is peculiarly human, does that mean that animals do not have a sense of humour?

It's a dog's life!

We simply do not know what the inner consciousness of animals is like. Chimpanzees have been taught to sign simple phrases and to count. This does show amazing intelligence, but they are not capable of abstract grammar. They hit a ceiling very quickly. Apes, dogs and dolphins, for example, can play, and be taught to do tricks. They have a sense of fun. Dogs detect when something is not as it should be, wagging tails, jumping and whining.

These might be the rudimentary roots of a sense of humour, but there is so much more going on in human laughter. We look out on the universe and see profundities.

What happens when we laugh?

Laughter is under the control of the more primitive parts of the brain, the 'old brain', which consists of the thalami and the hypothalamus. These govern reflex action and purely emotional behaviour. The cerebral cortex, conversely, deals with our rational ability.

Spasmodic contractions of the large and small facial muscles, with sudden relaxations of the diaphragm, in company with contractions of the larynx and the epiglottis.

This is a physical description of laughter. Put simply, this means that laughter involves breathing being interrupted by muscle tension and release.

Tickled pink!

The process can be triggered by physical actions such as tickling. It can also be the result of a joke – an abstract tale of complex, verbal associations. Just how the same process can be initiated by a simple reflex action or such a reasoning ability is beyond us. It is one of life's mysteries, as much as what the exact relationship between the mind and brain is.

Collapsing into laughter

Laughter involves tension being built up, which is released as we capitulate to the laugh. Yet *we collapse into laughter* – the 'I' is still reflectively involved when observing a humorous situation. There is reflection *and* reflex. Laughter feels so damned good because it is cathartic – it releases tensions and emotions, and relaxes muscles.

Laughter therapy

Laughter is good for the soul. Comedy is therapy. This is being utilized by some counsellors and clinics across the world. There is a National Health Laughter Clinic in Birmingham! A laughter-therapy session can involve clients lying on their backs, heads touching, in a circle. They start to laugh. The communal nature of the event gets them going, until there are belly laughs and the tears flow.

Laughter clinics

Practitioners are quick to list the health benefits.

effects to the circulatory system

the respiratory system

the immune system

stimulation of facial, abdominal and chest muscles (as in jogging)

release of adrenalin, with the possible release of endorphins from the hypothalamus and enkephalins (a pair with narcotic properties that help depression and reduce pain).

Clowning about

Another form of laughter therapy is seen in some hospital wards in the United States. Clowns are hired or even, sometimes, doctors dress up and perform slapstick acts and stand-up routines in the wards. It raises morale and has a psychological impact on health. Some hospitals have a comedy room, showing the cable Comedy Channel.

It's OK... stand back... I'm a clown!

Why Do We Laugh?

Reverse engineering

Scientists wonder about the origin and purpose of humanity's sense of humour. One way of analysing this is to engage in some reverse engineering. This involves looking back at animal behaviour – particularly that of human-related, higher mammals – and seeing correlations between their behaviour in the wild and our more sophisticated social interactions. This derives from an evolutionary perspective, and looks at the survival value that humour might have. If anything has developed within us, then it is expected to have a utility function.

Zoo time

Chimpanzees and gorillas are close relations of human beings. They reveal behaviour that is close to humour.

They smile, stretching their lips and baring their teeth in an action that is physiologically close to that of human smiling. The purpose of the smile depends upon the context. On one hand, a group of apes might be play fighting, showing that they are not a real threat to each other. On the other hand, the bared teeth might become aggressive, as one ape gets into a stand-off with another. This smile might be brought on by a reflex action when an ape is tickled in rough-and-tumble play.

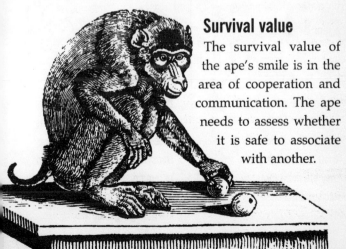

Survival value

The survival value of the ape's smile is in the area of cooperation and communication. The ape needs to assess whether it is safe to associate with another.

The flirt

Skills of communication and cooperation are just as vital for human beings. Consider the following situations:

Flirting is a game played to establish boundaries. People need to establish that they are not a threat to each other.

If a joke falls upon deaf ears, or a flirtatious remark is seen as rude, then a boundary is being transgressed. A boss might wish to remain aloof, for humour is democratic. It is inherently social, like eating together.

What emerges?

To sum up human humour merely by comparison to the apes is like describing the latest I-MAC computer in terms of the functions of one of the old Sinclair ZX Spectrum computers. Long and complicated code strings and commands have been superseded by visual icons, clicking with a mouse and graphics packages which allow 3-D simulation and many other whizzy functions. We seem to be light years away.

It's absurd!

Humans are capable of abstract thought and have a heightened sense of self-awareness and irony. Their use of sophisticated wordplay goes way beyond the antics and smiles of their fellow simians, as satire, political jokes and the alternative, zany humour of absurd TV shows. Human humour is an *emergence*, to use a philosopher's term. It is something that has come from simpler roots, but has blossomed and grown beyond all expectations.

The pie in the face

We laugh at the clown taking a custard pie in the face. Slapstick gets laughs at the expense of someone else's downfall, but the banana skin and the pie are harmless. It is all play. Likewise, some film violence that makes us laugh is also harmless. To take one example, the scene in *Indiana Jones and the Raiders of the Lost Ark* in which Indy is faced by the elaborate movements of a scimitar-wielding assassin raises the roof when Indy simply takes out a gun and shoots him.

Aggression

But does humour thrive on aggressive instincts? A purely evolutionary model cannot get away from this.

It has been said that the first clown was the caveman who pushed his axe into another's head and laughed, for he had the victory. Satire and slapstick do depend upon a degree of aggression. Mockery belittles the recipient, and helps the comedian's dignity. Hence the racist's jokes.

Play along

Let's not forget play, though. Mimetic play with toy guns might be a way of helping children to come to terms with the way the world is. We must not assume that they are learning how to be aggressive. It is a far cry from a toy gun to a real one.

The Indiana Jones scene mentioned earlier was not about the relishing of vulgar violence. We did not find a man being shot, with all the spurting blood and oozing guts, funny. It was the slapstick absurdity of the whole action (and the violence was off-screen).

And perhaps humour has a healing power, a healthy, holistic function that goes way beyond mere mockery.

Between the Apes and the Angels

Bottoms up!

Some of us enjoy coarse humour. For all our lofty philosophizing, we enjoy a bit of rough. From the wild antics and dares of a stag night to the toilet humour in the school playground or in student rags such as *Viz*, people guffaw along. If we put on a disapproving face, we might still be dying to laugh, inside! Perhaps we just never grow up.

Earthed

Maybe it's nothing to do with growing up; perhaps it's just about being human. We have bodies through which we move, feel and do things. We are embodied beings. Crude, scatological humour earths us, puts us in touch with reality and keeps our feet on the ground. Bodily 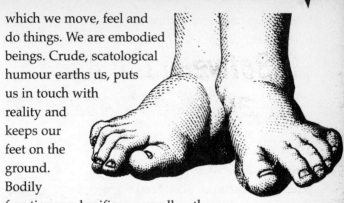 functions and orifices, as well as the sex drive, are part and parcel of being human – *alive*.

Laughing yourself alive

There is a story told of Iambe and Demeter in ancient Greek mythology. Demeter, the earth goddess, was in mourning. The lord of Hades had taken her daughter, Persephone, and she was inconsolable. She wandered in search of the girl, robed and disguised as an old woman. She sat down on a rock called Unsmiling, and would not speak.

Iambe found her and tried to raise her spirits.

Eventually, Iambe let forth a torrent of expletives and obscenities, gushing crude humour forth until the 'old hag' started to laugh – a deep belly laugh up from the gut – and she got up from the rock and left Unsmiling behind. Demeter was in touch with her body, in touch with life again.

Stick 'em up!

Ribaldry and crude jesting often focus on sex. The jester's stick and the Fool's pole carry phallic implications. Look at some classic Greek vases and see the rough and tumble with the enormous penises, or catch glimpses of padded bums and artificial phalluses worn by actors in an Aristophanes play.

'He carries Love before him like a staff.'

Jack and the stick

In the Jack cycle of tales (as in the beanstalk) one English variant has Jack with a singing bee, a magic fiddle that plays itself and a stick. He comes to woo the unsmiling princess who watches the bee, hears the fiddle and then falls about whooping with laughter when, with one command, 'Up stick and at 'em!' the stick was off, poking this one and that, prodding and knocking the local dignitaries! The king has promised his unsmiling daughter to the man who can make her laugh!

Let go!

In fact, this old tale carries a deep truth. People who are attracted to each other can make each other laugh. A woman's flick of the hair, throwing her head back and letting go in laughter is a sign of lowering the defences.

A woman blushing is suggestive of a sexually aroused state, as the skin behaves in a similar way: the cheeks are engorged with blood, the skin prickles and the temperature rises. Involuntary outbreaks of laughter are a further abandonment and exposure, as the body flips into reflex action and its muscle spasms mimic those of orgasm. The laughing mouth with its stretched lips is suggestive of the female genitalia.

Down the well

One of the ancient Greek philosophers was so fascinated by the stars that he spent his days looking up towards the heavens. Alone with his lofty thoughts, he went out walking one day and he fell down a well! He should have been looking where he was going!

What better way to sum up the human condition? Creatures of the primeval slime, made of the atoms and chemicals of the earth, defecating and aching, having sex and feeding, we are also rational beings. Our thoughts can dissect the universe and seek the Big Answers. How trapped we are, what a mixture of heaven and earth, apes and angels we!

Ghost in the machine

We are walking puzzles. Do we have immortal souls, or are we complex networks of brain stuff that fizzes with electricity and rushes chemical 'thoughts' around our heads? Is the mind a mere by-product of the working brain, destined to fade away when the body dies? Or are our minds something elusively sublime, intimately linked to our brains, yet separable?

There are no provable, definite answers to these questions. Different scientists and philosophers say different things. Perhaps our minds use our brains rather like TV signals are received by a TV set. Destroy the TV and the signals are still there, only we can't see or hear them. Maybe the mind is produced by the working brain, but is greater than the sum of its parts. This wonderful thing is then beyond the physical.

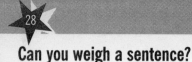

Can you weigh a sentence?

If you could measure the electrical current in the brain and the chemicals produced when you form a sentence, would this mean that you could weigh it? In one sense, yes, but this is a mechanistic and materialistic explanation, reducing our inner life and our abstract thoughts to mere brain stuff. Surely there is more to a sentence than that? Our words and thoughts carry the whole realm of human meaning within them.

Walking puzzles – alive, thinking and feeling. We are embodied beings, living in and through our skin, but aspiring to the stars. *And* we have a conscience, for even when we find some crude things funny, we might be ashamed about doing them ourselves.

What's so Funny?

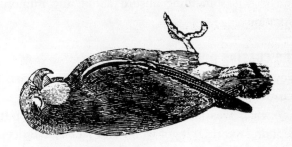

What makes us laugh?

What is funny about Monty Python's dead-parrot sketch? It is an absurd situation, with an unbelievable attempt to con the customer: 'No, no, it's resting, look!'... 'It's not pining. It's passed on. This parrot is no more. It has ceased to be. It's expired and gone to meet its maker. This is a late parrot. It's a stiff. Bereft of life, it rests in peace. If you hadn't nailed it to its perch, it would be pushing up the daisies. It's rung down the curtain and joined the choir invisible. This is an ex-parrot.'

The scholar John Southworth, in *Fools and Jesters at the English Court*, remarked, 'Humour consists essentially in a surprising juxtaposition of opposites.'

There is something absurd about any humorous situation.

The cussing parrot

Never mind the dead parrot, what about the cussing parrot?

A vicar was looking after a friend's parrot, but it kept on swearing. It got worse and worse, and deeply offended the Mothers' Union meeting. In desperation, he shoved it in the freezer to teach it a lesson. After a little while, he relented and pulled it out.

'Are you going to behave now?'

Extremely contrite, the parrot replied, 'Phew! You bet! If I was bad, what on earth did the chicken get up to?'

Silly, and all good fun. It amuses. Note the incongruity, the juxtaposition of parrot and frozen chicken.

Nobody expects…

'Nobody expects the Spanish Inquisition. Our chief weapon is surprise… surprise and fear… fear and surprise… our two weapons are fear and surprise… and ruthless efficiency.' Nobody expects the unexpected. If we saw the joke coming, we'd duck for cover. A good laugh is a surprise. Humour is a shake-up, a pie in the face.

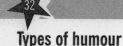

Types of humour

The parrot jokes were of benign, or consoling humour.
A good laugh. Period.

Wit involves more of the intellect, with
wordplay and the sharp riposte, but some
level of intellect and understanding is required
for any joke. Try telling the cussing-parrot
joke to some five-year-olds. How many will
get it?

Satire, according to the sociologist Peter Berger,
is 'the deliberate use of the comic for purposes
of attack'. This could be aggressive and
indiscriminate, ripping the P out of anyone and
everything, or it can be more principled,
exposing hypocrisy which deserves to be
exposed.

Burlesque describes a satirical drama,
caricaturing various people.

Slapstick is the pratfall of rough and tumble, the pie in the face, the practical joke of *Candid Camera* or *Beadle's About*.

Black humour is tragicomedy, defying the tragic with laughter as a distraction or in spite of the difficulty.

Farce is a drama/comedy sketch involving characters in ludicrous situations. Hence, to say something is a 'farcical event' is to point out how ludicrous it is.

Racist humour?

One controversial area is satirical issues involving racist attitudes. Take Johnny Spreight's *Till Death Us Do Part*, for example. This presented a racist bigot in such unflattering terms that we were supposed to laugh at Alf, not with him. Yet wasn't the irony lost on some, as they saw a funny guy on TV mouthing their attitudes and pet hates? The average *Sun* reader of the day did not get the irony. Neither did Mary Whitehouse! And stand-up comedians? Claims that Bernard Manning is not really being racist, he is just mocking the racists, wear a bit thin.

It's every c*** that I hate!

Journalist Howard Jacobson, in his book *Seriously Funny*, makes a plea for clemency for comedians like Manning, feeling that he lances a boil by getting his white audiences to let out their aggression. Others would say this only serves to inflame hatred. Whatever, Jacobson does point out that a touch of humour would have undermined Hitler's speeches.

Had Hitler come to the microphone in flying goggles, danced a little on his toes, and assured the assembled half million, 'I'm not a racist – I just hate every c***,' instead of declaiming with that terrible univocal monotony, 'If we do not take steps etc., etc.,' his audiences in Nuremberg would have responded differently, and so, probably, would history.

If we can laugh at ourselves, we don't take ourselves so seriously.

Don't mention the war!

Self-parody hits the mark, as in *Fawlty Towers*. In the episode 'The Germans', Basil makes a complete ass of himself in his attempts to not embarrass his German guests:

'Listen… don't mention the war!… So that's two eggs mayonnaise, a prawn Goebbels, a Hermann Goering and four Colditz salads.'

He ends up a goose-stepping, gibbering wreck in a parody of an apoplectic Hitler. Thus, Naziism is attacked as pathetic, as is the myopic cultural awareness of middle-class Britain.

Goodness, gracious me!

Such healthy humour is also in the Asian hit comedy series, *Goodness, Gracious Me!* This pokes fun not only at their own kind – their hang-ups and class barriers ('That's Indian!'), but at the English too.

Asian travellers in the UK shooting a travelogue, or, 'Let's have an English!' as well as the stay-at-home, all in the extended family antics of the Indian mother who wants to cook and celebrate everything at home: 'You want Paris? We could do it better at home!' This is enlightened humour, for everyone ends up laughing at themselves. And that helps us to be friends.

It's magic!

There are overlaps between all the types of humour, for the comic involves a sudden and unexpected shift in our perception of reality. It's like a magic act, as a rabbit is pulled out of a hat.

Consoling humour is like white magic, perhaps, as

it is gentle and soothing. The tragicomic and the satirical are more biting, grappling with the dark side of life, and are like blacker, more potent magic. Laughter is the 'magic' power we possess in our souls.

Dying to laugh

In the days of the Raj, a British officer lay wounded on the battlefield. A spear was sticking out of his chest. A soldier rushed up to him:

'Does it hurt?'

'Only when I laugh!'

We don't expect the punchline. We don't see it coming, and this silly situation is a piece of biting satire, too, as it pokes fun at the stiff-upper-lip British. It does hurt some people to laugh, at first, because it means they can't hide away behind their 'mask'. When you laugh – truly laugh, freely laugh – you have to be yourself.

Open the Door!

Ecstacy!

The sociologist Peter Berger says that human beings are *ecstatic* creatures – we stand out of our skins. We are bodily organisms, but we are also aware of *having* a body. It is as though the conscious ego can stand apart from the body, and be aware of its existence.

Out of the ordinary

Laughter can take us out of the ordinary, beyond normality and routine, to see afresh. We stop, and transcend the moment. The same can be true of any aesthetic or religious experience, in art, music or before a numinous beauty perceived through nature.

It is like an alternative view of reality – the rousing sonata, the tree in the mist. How rushed our modern lives can be, from one project to the next, never far from the office via the internet and the mobile phone. Anything that breaks open a crack into our inner selves, that makes us stop and listen, is good and healthy.

Open the trapdoor!

In German thought, humour is compared to a stage where various trapdoors and objects can appear out of the blue and interrupt the normal play-acting. It makes us trip and tumble.

At the punchline of a joke, our world opens up and what we take for granted falls away. There is a moment of euphoria, of transcendence, as we step out of ourselves. We relax into a joke, and accept its reality, however briefly. It is like taking a holiday, for on holiday we rest, unwind and behave differently – wildly even, especially if far from home. Then we think more clearly, seeing what we should do.

Homo ludens

Humans are playful beings, *Homo ludens*. Besides sports to help us unwind or provide a challenge, we like all kinds of little psychological and sociological games. Rituals and rites are a form of play, as we enter into a symbolic drama and act out a role, a persona, looking askance and afresh. We can express deep feelings in symbol and actions. Think of the need many felt to do *something* when Diana died – the teddy bears, the messages, the tons of flowers and the many candles, flickering into the night.

Memorial tree

Or another time, when a group of teenagers gathered around a newly planted tree in memory of one of their friends, killed so tragically early in a car accident. The tree was blessed with holy water, a symbol suggestive of life.

Flowers and candles were placed around it, as they chatted and hugged for hours. As one said later, 'We'll return to that tree when we're seventy!'

A minor key

Stepping outside everyday reality can be, in Peter Berger's phrase, a 'sign of transcendence'. In a minor key, in a small way, this is the different angle on reality, the release of the joke, the escape from the humdrum and the power of the present moment. Having a good laugh can make us feel so *alive*, as we experience raw existence, living for the moment.

Existentialist philosophers such as Jean-Paul Sartre have told us how special it is to be, simply to BE. Sartre famously said, 'Existence precedes essence.' What we are not are static, abstract somethings, but living, moving, feeling beings... BEING.

A major key

Laughter opens up new possibilities. Things don't have to be the same any more. They can change! Just as we are ecstatic beings, we can look askance at our world and say, 'Thus have we made it, thus can we remake it.' It is in our hands. We are not trapped in impersonal forces and processes. Mockery and satire are such important political weapons because they open the door of change. They challenge, undress pomposity and question authority. Cant and hypocrisy are paraded for all to see.

If people dare laugh at facism, then consider how silly the jackboots look. Those apparently insecure men seem to take themselves far too seriously – all those buttons and belts, tch!

Tears and smiles

Animals do not weep, and neither do they smile as humans do. Tears and laughter are both gifts given to humanity. To be able to despair, and to hope, is to be human and alive. We can stand outside the processes of nature and society and can wonder, cry, laugh, protest, shout and dance for change. A good joke opens up new worlds.

The Danish philosopher, Søren Kierkegaard, once remarked that humour was incognito faith, the

existential threshold of the great leap of trust in transcendence and unseen purpose. It was at the verge of religious faith… interesting.

Language games

We are more than atoms and chemicals, for we are preciously human. There are things that can be felt, but not analysed, sung, but not spoken, danced or painted, but not demonstrated in logic. The philosopher Ludwig Wittgenstein was right when he saw that humans had many different 'language games', each with their own rules. We are multi-layered creatures. Don't be a reductionist, be a holist! Laugh all the way to the bank.

Fools Rush In...

Who were the Fools?

Emperors, kings, chieftains and pharaohs have all had their Fools. We mustn't think that it was only the Medieval kings. Clowning around at court goes back a long way. They have been called by different names, had different outfits and equipment, but they have all been Fools at heart.

Fools had a talent to amuse, stand-up comedians of old or circus clowns who were patronized by a ruler. They were there to entertain, to make the Big Man laugh! But there was more to them than that – they could be advisers and semi-prophetic figures, cutting to the quick and revealing the hearts of their masters. Sometimes, there could be religious and cultic functions ascribed to them, too.

Getting away with murder?

The Renaissance scholar Erasmus once said, 'indeed, the words that would cost a wise man his life are surprisingly enjoyable when uttered by a clown. For truth has a genuine power to please if it manages not to give offence, but this is something the gods have granted only to Fools.'

Twisty Pole's wisdom

There is a tale of an ancient Chinese Fool called 'Twisty Pole'. His emperor wanted to lacquer the entire length of the Great Wall of China! No one dared oppose him, until Twisty Pole said,

'That's a splendid idea. Lacquer the Great Wall all smooth and shiny, then it will be too slippery for any invaders to climb over it. Now, let's get down to the practical side of the job. The lacquering is easy enough, but building a drying room may present a problem or two!'

Silence. Then a slow smile spread over the emperor's face and Twisty Pole burst out laughing. The wit had deflected the emperor's anger and punctured his pomposity. The emperor was able to laugh at himself!

Alter egos

Sometimes, the Fool was a kind of alter ego of the ruler. He was more than the fall guy; he was the foil, the mirror image that enabled the ruler to see himself more clearly. It was a team, and older societies saw this as divinely inspired.

The ruler was Order, and the Fool was Chaos. One controlled and planned, and one was unpredictable, always doing a trick or pulling the carpet from under someone. Life, the cosmos, was a delicate balance of

Order and Chaos, and thus it had been established at the creation. Creation myths always speak of the gods or God mastering the stormy forces of chaos, sometimes pictured as dark waters (as in the Bible) or as a great monster.

It's stifling in here!

In society, too much order stifles creativity and spontaneity. Life can't always be planned. John Lennon once said, 'Life is what happens to you when you're making other plans.' Too much anarchy leads to disorder, confusion and danger. Life has to be a delicate balance.

It is often noted that when the Greek philosopher Plato wrote his magnum opus, *The Republic*, giving his blueprint for the ideal society run by philosophers, he had no room for the poets in it. They were too emotional and uncontrollable, and inspiration was seen as suspect. You can't pin that down! Needless to say, he had no room for the Fools, either.

Gifts of the gods

In ancient Egypt, the pharaohs had pygmies as Fools. They called them the *danga* people, and they came from south of the Nile – probably African pygmies. They were known for their dancing skills and had a sacred function, dancing a representation of the rising of the sun each day. A curious text shows how they were deeply immersed in the religious rituals of the time. In this pyramid text, the dead pharaoh seeks to persuade Ra, the sun god, to speedily take him to heaven by imitating his *danga*, his pygmy Fool. He actually announces himself as the *danga*, pretending to be him, 'that pygmy of the dances of god who diverts the god in front of his great throne'. Thus we see the alter ego, the Siamese-twin effect of ruler and Fool.

Dwarves and simpletons

The idea of having a dwarf as a Fool was adopted by the Normans, and at various times in the Middle Ages. The Bayeux tapestry shows a dwarf Fool, Turold.

The simpleton, the village idiot, the mentally subnormal, also found a role as a Fool in some courts. The unpretentious honesty and happy demeanour of such people made them ideal candidates. Here, we see something of the outsider at work, the social freak and outcast evoking awe and curiosity.

Mr Nobody

Fools were outside the social hierarchy. In the Middle Ages they simply did not fit into the feudal system of serfs, freemen and nobles. They had no bearing, no social status. Classless, they stood on the fringes and were only present because a ruler tolerated them, and,

often, bestowed huge favours upon them – favours which could also be taken away. In Latin texts the Fools are described as *nebulo* – worthless. Their very social invisibility allowed them to come and go, and gave them freedom to say things no one else dared. It was not above their station, for they had no above or below; everything was on the level!

Moving on up?

A Fool *could* leave his profession and slot into the social hierarchy. This happened with Rayer in twelfth-century England. Something happened on a pilgrimage to Rome, and upon his return, he joined the Austin canons. They were a creative, reforming monastery and he took something of his spirit of play into his life as a monk. He founded St Bartholomew's Priory and Hospital (which became 'Bart's Hospital'). He played the role of the idiot, drawing groups of children and servants around him. This was not idle buffoonery, but playful compassion, and he said, 'They that are foolish and feeble in the world's reputation our Lord chooses to confound the might of the world.'

All dressed up...

A Fool dressed differently in the different ages. The Medieval Fool wore a jester's cap with bells and pointed shoes. A club or stick of some kind was also carried. The marotte was a stick with a miniature Fool's head on it; alternatively, the stick might have had a pig's bladder on the end. These 'weapons' had a hint of aggression, though playful, as the Fool japed and poked and prodded people. He attacked where his companion was weak, showing up hypocrisy and exposing stupidity. Sometimes, the Fool carried large wafers, juggling with them as mock hosts from the mass.

Danse macabre

The Medieval *danse macabre* at All Hallows utilized the Fool in the streets. Here, people dressed as Fools and mocked people dressed as Death, and then Death, too, put on a jester's cap and danced along, mocking any dignitaries he met along the way. The world went topsy-turvy for a time as people celebrated the ridiculous.

The Feast of Fools

So valued was the Fool's role in Medieval society that the church held the Feast of Fools, in which a boy bishop was elected, from 6 December (the feast of St Nicholas) through to New Year. On New Year's Eve in the cathedrals, the junior clergy rose up and shouted 'Put down! Put down!' at the verse of the Magnificat: 'He has put down the mighty from their seats and exalted the humble.'

Burlesque followed as they took over the service and an ass was brought in, carrying a mother holding a baby (recalling the flight into Egypt of the Christ child) as they chanted 'Up, Sir Ass and sing!' The priest

celebrating mass had to bray like a donkey at various points, and three times at the dismissal!

This larking and tomfoolery was a spiritual act – it enacted the truth of the Magnificat in which the humble were exalted.

Literary Fools

The most famous literary Fool is in Shakespeare's *King Lear*. The mad king cries out, 'Who is it that can tell me who I am?' It is the jesting Fool who not only can, but dares to, the alter ego of Lear and the one who can cross the boundaries of class and convention. We find the wise idiot again in Dostoevsky's *The Idiot*, with Prince Myshkin, and in film, with Peter Sellars as the simple gardener in *Being There*. Then there is Eddie Murphy in *The Holy Man*, striding out along the US highways in his white robe and with bare feet. In one scene he has nearly everyone in the United States rushing outside to contemplate a patch of grass.

The Idiot

At the start of Dostoevsky's *The Idiot*, Prince Myshkin arrives in Russia from Sweden, where he has been convalescing. Dressed in a foreign cape, looking ill and carrying his belongings in a bundle, he causes people to look askance at him. He arrives at the house of General Yepanchin, whose wife is a distant relation. The household servant does not know what to make of this unexpected visitor. The prince does not follow the usual protocol or respectful etiquette. When ushered into another room he replies, 'If you don't mind... I'd rather wait here with you. What am I going to do there alone by myself?'

'I'm sorry, sir, but I'm afraid you can't possibly stay in the ante-room, because you are a visitor, or, in other words, a guest.'

The servant's suspicions grow and he wonders if he is a scrounger.

'Have you really come – er – from abroad, sir?' he asked almost involuntarily, and – stopped short in confusion; what he wanted perhaps to ask was, 'Are you really Prince Myshkin?'

'Yes, I've come straight from the station. I think what you wanted to ask me was whether I was really Prince Myshkin, but did not ask it out of politeness.'

'H'm,' the astonished servant grunted.

The clowns around us

Gradually, as society changed and rulers became more constitutional and democratic, the need for the ruler's alter ego foundered. The court Fool vanished, but tomfoolery lived on, dissipated in the clowns and players in society, and later the cartoonists, stand-up comedians, satirists and Chaplins of the entertainment world. Some of this is just for fun, but the folly of the comedian can also be sharply wise, exposing double standards in governments and calling absurdity by its name. Totalitarian regimes imprison their Fools and try to gag them. They seem to take everything so, so deadly seriously.

The clowns within

Inside each of us is the emotional self and the rational self – Dionysus and Apollo, to borrow from Greek myth. Too much of one and we are out of kilter – the silly buffoon who takes nothing seriously, or the anally retentive perfectionist who has had a humour bypass. We need balance, equilibrium. Jung drew four-pointed mandalas, depicting the opposites within us in tension, and transactional analysis speaks of the child, parent and adult within each of us. The Fool is the child, innocent and honest, seeing through hypocrisy and dancing with glee at the sun glistening on the bluebells. Free the Fool within!

Tickled into life!

The story is told of Harlequin being depressed and deciding to kill himself. His suicide instrument was a large feather; he tried to tickle himself to death! After some minutes, he was laughing so much that he stopped wanting to die, and was in love with life again. Laughter raises the spirits.

Laughter After Auschwitz

Smiling in the face of pain?

T.W. Adorno wrote, 'To write poetry after Auschwitz is barbaric.' Such a horror, such a scale of human suffering, cannot be shut out by carrying on with life. And yet, life has to go on. It just has to, and would the victims have wanted it any other way (if only to see children smiling again)?

Laughter can be so shallow and frivolous that to speak of it in the face of suffering sounds facile. Laughter can be medicine for the soul, though, and promise better things.

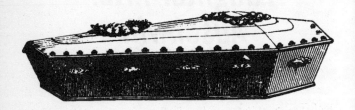

Gallows humour

One attendant at a crematorium eats his sandwiches while reading *The Sun* newspaper. This is spread out over the coffin in the back room. Irreverent, or a natural coping mechanism?

One obvious way of using laughter when in a painful situation is as a distraction – just like the soldiers who jest in the shell hole, the doctors who quip before surgery, the funeral directors who joke behind the scenes. It takes your mind off the grim stuff. But there's more…

Jewish humour

The Jews have had more than their fair share of suffering throughout their history. After being beaten about by the Romans, the Christian church called them 'Christ-killers' and laid the foundations for the gross acts of anti-Semitism that followed. Never mind the fact that it was the *Romans* and a few of the Jewish *leaders* who did for Jesus, it took until the middle of the last century for there to be any official church apologies.

There are some remarkable examples of the use of humour by this ancient and noble race, as they coped with adversity.

A little bit of yiddish in my soul

Yiddish developed from the mixture of German, Polish and Hebrew being spoken by European Jewry in the Middle Ages. The official prayers were in Hebrew, but off-stage comments could be made in Yiddish. So, 'You have chosen us from among the nations,' could be read at morning prayer, with an acerbic aside in Yiddish, 'Why did you have to pick on the Jews?' Yiddish, the amalgam language, gathered words and idioms from various lands as Jews wandered from place to place and were exiled. The Yiddish writer I.L. Peretz states that the language reflects this constant movement and persecution, carrying its 'precious jewels' of Jewish tears.

Fiddler on the Roof

The characters in the film *Fiddler on the Roof* were based upon the plays of Sholem Aleichem. These were set in Tsarist Russia when many Jews were being persecuted and thrown off their land. There, Jews had a bitter sense of the ironic, celebrating festivals in a foreign country, landless and wandering. How odd they must have felt sitting in their temporary shelters to celebrate Succoth, outside, in the cold autumn, commemorating the time when the Hebrews wandered in the Sinai desert.

Sholem Aleichem wanted to give a voice to a rejected people, and to create laughter in a wretched world. His character, Tevye, is the ironic narrator, determined to survive against all odds.

Smash your own windows!

The last Tevye story deals with the conditions of a Russian pogrom. The May laws ordered that all Jews must leave rural areas. Tevye comes home to find the whole village assembled outside his house, The elder, Paparilo, tells Tevye that they must have a pogrom:

> 'We've nothing against you personally... We'll have to smash your windows at least, because if anyone passing through here sees there's been no pogrom yet, we'll be in hot waters ourselves.'

Paparilo muses that as they're Tevye's windows, he might as well smash them himself! Later, dreaming about the Messiah arriving on a white horse, Tevye hears the village policeman arriving on his horse. He has brought an order of expulsion. It is useless to argue against the law. He sells up and moves his family out. One of them, Chava, had converted to Orthodox Christianity, but returns to be exiled with the rest of them. Chava declares, 'is Tevye right or not when he says that there's a great God above and that a man must never lose heart while he lives? And that's especially true of a Jew… Anyone can be a goy, but a Jew must be born one.'

Faith or resignation? Irony or belief? The sense of irony is underscored by Tevye comparing his journey to that of Abraham, except that the father of the faith was being sent to the Promised Land. Where was Tevye going to go to?

In the midst of suffering, cause a smile, raise the spirits. That's Yiddish humour.

Bitter hearts

Robert Bober's novel, *What News of the War*, is a moving testament to the Holocaust survivors. He sets the action in post-war Paris, in a tailor's shop where Jews who avoided deportation, and returnees from the camps both work, side by side. It is a cutting-room world in the Rue de Turenne. Slowly, smiles are returning again, as they are able to joke with each other *and* about their past. Maurice Abramowicz is nicknamed 'Abramauschwitz' by fellow Jews. Leon the presser works part time in the avant garde Yiddish theatre (where some of Sholem Aleichem's plays are performed). He pulls pranks all the time, but when he first came back, he didn't dare!

The characters are learning to laugh again *because they are learning to live again*, but they cannot, dare not, forget their painful experiences, which are interlaced as flashbacks throughout the book.

How can people come back laughing? Some still cannot.

Madame Sarah cannot laugh, and she cannot bring herself to praise anyone or anything. When she is given a glass of cool beer in the cutting shop she patronizes, she says in disgust, 'It tastes like piss!' even though all present know it is the finest beer available. You see, she lost her husband, who was the love of her life, and the lights have gone out. When life collapses like that, who wouldn't give in? But if you don't laugh, all you can do is cry.

Life is Beautiful

Roberto Benigni's award-winning film, *Life is Beautiful*, caused controversy before and after it was released. What should we make of a black comedy about the Holocaust, the Shoah? Benigni plays a comedian who is sent to one of the camps with his young son. He takes up a ridiculous game of pretence, trying to convince his little boy that the Nazis are only playing. If they follow the bizarre rules of the 'game', then they will be all right. This gets harder and harder to maintain as so much cruelty goes on around them. Eventually, the father is killed – out of sight of the boy – and the son does not know what has happened. Thus the game continues.

It is far from frivolous, and despite lots of humour, is very poignant in the end.

'Lick my heart…'

Before people saw the film, many feared it would be trivializing, rather like the TV series *Allô, Allô*, taking off the French resistance and the Gestapo with phoney accents. Writing in *The Independent* before he had seen the film, Howard Jacobson spoke about his hopes for it as a Jew. He quoted a line from the film *Shoah*, where one of the victims says, 'If you could lick my heart, it would poison you.' Just like Madame Sarah. Jacobson retorts,

> But what good is served by taking a poisonous heart into eternity?… It's (comedy) province is pain and trouble… Why send an ambulance to a house where nobody is ill?… Laughter proclaims life, even in the face of death.

Redemptive myths

Jacobson raised a searching question about humour, Jews and the Shoah. He comments on the absence of any redeeming myth in Judaism in the wake of the Shoah. There is a vacuum, except, perhaps, for the State of Israel. The 'Land' is idolized, defended, and terrible extremes tolerated, because it is a safe haven after so much terror and displacement throughout the last century and earlier. This isolationist, defensive attitude is no way to build a society, though. It breeds madmen like Baruch Goldstein, who fired his machine-gun into a crowded mosque during Friday prayers in 1994, or it makes soldiers brutal with Palestinians, or rude and offensive to travellers who might have the wrong visa in their passport. The nation needs to relax and smile again. Laughter and redemption – comedy and hope – are so intimately linked.

Songs of Zion

Laughter and redemption, songs and hope – these themes are often linked in the Bible. Think of the lament of the exiles – the Jews who had been taken captive to Babylon – in Psalm 137:

> *By the rivers of Babylon we sat down;*
> *there we wept when we remembered Zion.*
> *On the willows near by we hung up our harps.*
> *Those who captured us told us to sing;*
> *they told us to entertain them;*
> *'Sing us a song about Zion.'*
> *How can we sing a song to the Lord in a foreign*
> *land?*

The heartbroken and the captives cannot sing, or laugh. Perhaps time is a healer, and the first smile the hint of a new dawn.

The Divine Comedy

A religious joke

At a church meeting, an emotional woman stood up in a time of open prayer and raised her hands to the heavens. She cried tears of joy and said, 'I thank you, Lord, that last night I was lost in sin in the arms of Satan, but tonight I have seen the light, and I am safe in the arms of Jesus!' A man leaned forward and tapped her on the shoulder. 'Pssst! How about being in my arms tomorrow night, darling?'

Should believers find this offensive? Perhaps religious folk *need* to laugh at themselves sometimes. Look at the special, metaphorical language used by the woman. How true it is that 'church speak' can be odd and gobbledygook to outsiders. To reverse the situation, it's a bit like sending a vicar into a bingo hall.

Religion on the telly

Too often, religion sees laughter as frivolous. It is seen as shallow.

Some 'tut-tut' about programmes like *The Vicar of Dibley* when they haven't even seen them. Religion is not a suitable subject for humour! In fact, besides being a very funny sitcom, Dawn French plays the title role with considerable sensitivity at times, and the programme touches upon some deep issues. There was the one about the window – how much should be spent on church decor and how much on the poor? Then, what about the one where people learned how to say farewell to a silly old woman who was dying?

Father Ted was zanier, and had Roman Catholics divided into two camps. Some saw it as scandalous, but others loved it – including a large number of Catholic priests! It did not mock the faith at all, but merely the church subculture of Ireland.

The fools and the wise

The Bible often polarizes the 'fool' and the 'wise man'.
The book of Proverbs has this as a constant refrain, and
one of the psalms says,

> *'Fools say to themselves,*
> *"There is no God."*
> *They are all corrupt.'*
>
> Psalm 14:1

By 'fool', the scriptures mean something different from
the court Fools who were sharp witted and often told
the truth when no one else dared to do so. The biblical
fool was a waster, a genuine idiot and an all-round
unwise person such as the dole-queue scrounger who
drinks it all away. There is a type of shallow humour; it
is true that there is nothing more annoying than
someone who always makes light of things, but there is
more to humour than that. Humour can have depths,
and speak of hope, love, healing and redemption.

In God's image?

The scriptures also speak of humans as being made 'in the image of God', a technical term that means on the inside, not the outside. God doesn't look like us, but we share inner spirit: character, morals, creativity and reason.

If a sense of humour is so precious, and unique to human beings, then there is something of God in this too. He has given us the gift of laughter, and perhaps it is good to offer praises, sometimes, with a smile on our faces. Laughter is not always frivolous. And why shouldn't we laugh at religion? Believers can get ahead of their station, and full of bigoted ideas. If you make a fanatic laugh, he or she finds balance again, and sees how stupid they are sounding!

Awareness of our own failings, and the redemptive nature of laughter, should be key themes in any faith. And Jesus…? Imagine the following scene…

The stand-up comedian

A nightclub. Two bouncers took a break and stood at the back of the smoky hall. Reg slipped his hands into his pockets and pulled out a packet of salt 'n' vinegar crisps. Ted nudged him and the packet was offered.

'Who's next, then?'

'Jewish bloke.'

'Not another one – we had all those fiddlers, tailors and clowns last week.'

'The programme says this one's a bit different.'

Reg put on his glasses and flicked through the programme.

'Here we go... a Ben Elton style delivery with a John Cleese sense of the absurd, the perfect timing of this man shows that the jokes are on us when we least expect it. Fast and frantic, but with a biblical twist.'

'The Bible – that's bound to be boring, innit?'

The lights go down and a hush falls on the place. A tall, brown-skinned man rides in on a donkey, with long, flowing robe and a towel around his shoulder.

'Hello and good evening. My name is... Oh, come

on, you've seen me before, haven't you? You know, the face that is on a thousand windows, not to mention the odd duster or two?'

A ripple of applause and laughter passed through the audience.

'I was thinking of coming in a Rolls Royce tonight, as befitting my status as Lord of the universe, but I thought this looked better.'

Jesus got off the donkey and walked up to the edge of the stage.

'I want to walk about in my world and meet you, take a look at things from your point of view – because you know what they say about a rich man?'

Jesus walked off-stage and brought a camel back on.

'I'd like a volunteer from the audience for this next gag... yes, you, madam!'

A young woman jumped up onto the stage. Jesus took a needle out of his bumbag.

'One ordinary, average needle. Would you care to show that to the audience?'

The young woman held it up.

'Now, I'd like you to push that camel through the eye of that needle!'

She walked around the camel, looking at the needle. She giggled and shook her head. She stood by its head as it made disgusting noises which made her jump.

'I can't! It's impossible!'

'Quite right, madam! It's as hard for a rich man to enter the kingdom of heaven as it is for a camel to pass through the eye of a needle! Thank you.'

Take out the cork!

Jesus as a stand-up comic? The little foray into alternative comedy above is not meant to be disrespectful to anyone's beliefs. It is meant to draw out the subversive and ironic humour that Jesus used in the gospel stories. He had an acerbic wit that attacked cant and hypocrisy wherever he found it. It was the self-righteous who suffered the edge of his tongue, the legalistic Pharisees and the proudly pious. We can get so full of ourselves and puffed up with pride – take out the cork!

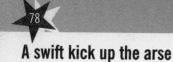

A swift kick up the arse

Humour is essential to a healthy spiritual development. Zen Buddhism is shot through with it, larking around to teach people to be humble and true to themselves. When one monk asked a master how to find enlightenment, he was kicked up the backside.

Seeing reality in a mirror

Humour holds a mirror up to ourselves, and we see our imperfections. It is the pious zealots who condemn others for they are humourless, and do not see their own projections and reflections in those whom they condemn. We have to laugh, or we'd go crazy! As Rabbi Lionel Blue says, 'Don't take it too heavy, dear! Don't take it too heavy!' Can you laugh at yourself?

The scouring pad

Rabbi Lionel Blue relishes the Jewish community's wealth of anti-Rabbi jokes, for these put a halt to his hubris, and bring him down to earth as a fellow human being.

There was the young rabbi, for example, who preached what he thought was a brilliant Atonement Day service. One old man snored all the way through. He woke him up and said, 'How could you have missed my sermon?' The old man looked at the young man and replied, 'Rabbi, to sleep through your sermon, that shows how much I trust you!' Lionel Blue comments, 'Humour can scour away and get to sins which the greatest sermons never reach.'

Christ the clown

Jesus played out something of the Fool's role, being 'in your face', subverting cherished ideas, and using wild humour to make his point. Even his parables form part of a comic tradition, for these draw the listener into a false sense of security and then deliver their punchlines, such as the Good Samaritan and the message of 'Who is my neighbour?' The punchline makes you see that a member of a despised race is actually the hero of the story.

In the musical *Godspell*, Jesus is dressed up as a clown. This caused offence when it was first performed, but people missed the point. Clowns knock the stuffing out of us and the truth into us!

Holy Fools

Jesus stood in a long line of Holy Fools in Judaism, going back to the Old Testament prophets. Isaiah went naked and barefoot for three years; Jeremiah walked around town with a wooden ox's yoke about his neck; Ezekiel ate excrement. These were all symbolic gestures, getting the message across in odd and graphic ways that the populace could not ignore. It was street theatre, with the effect of 'making strange' so beloved of the playwright Brecht.

Preaching to the birds

St Francis of Assisi is a good example of a Holy Fool after the time of Jesus. He gave up everything, stripping off his clothes in the marketplace and handing them back to his father. He embraced poverty and laughed and sang with the joy of God. He would dance and play the fiddle to cheer up his brothers, and he even preached to the birds.

Dead dogs and flatulence

The sixth-century St Simeon was a former hermit who wandered around teasing people endlessly. He threw nuts at people during church services, and ran naked into the women's section at the bathhouse. He once tied a dead dog onto his robe and dragged it around the town for the day. His pièce de résistance was to eat copious amounts of beans on fast days, with predictably loud results! Was he holy or mad? Perhaps he was fed up of fleeing from his body and the world, and wanted to teach people how to laugh again, for that gets you in touch with the earth so superbly.

Blood on your hands!

St Basil the Blessed once confronted Ivan the Terrible. The madman had just returned from one of his massacres, and the saint invited him to eat raw meat and blood. This was during the Orthodox Lent, when no meat was to be eaten. Ivan tried to be pious and refused, until Basil pointed out that he had not shown such qualms at shedding innocent blood during Lent, and he looked up at the sky, saying that he could see all the souls of those he had killed. Ivan, terrified, stopped the executions.

Jesus never laughed?!?

St John Chrysostom said that Jesus never laughed, for he was the perfect man. Strange, for this old saint had a lot of wise things to say, but this time he really goofed. It is true that it nowhere says, explicitly, that Jesus laughed in the gospels, but it does say that he wept when one of his friends died. Remember the strong link between tears and joy – you can't do one if you can't manage the other. He also exhibited quite a humour.

Jesus was able to accept the outsiders and the unloved – the prostitutes and the lepers – and make them his disciples. When you can laugh, you can cry. When you can laugh, you can love, and accept others, with all their faults.

Joker in the pack

Jesus entered Jerusalem as its coming king on a donkey. Where was the glorious chariot or stallion? A donkey? It is a silly, humble beast, speaking to us of tacky seaside holidays and children's rides. Jesus paraded in high-camp melodrama!

Some of the sayings of Jesus reveal a gutsy, zany humour too. He told people not to bother with a splinter in someone else's eye when they had a great big log in their own! He used absurd comparisons like this to create incongruities, showing up hypocrisy in others. Rather Pythonesque, really.

Pious prats

So where did Chrysostom get his silly ideas from? When Christianity moved out into the Roman empire, it met with philosophies and attitudes that were deep seated and traditional. These stated that the passions were to be kept under strict control, for reason was the most important thing, and following your emotions clouded this. This came from philosophers of old, such as Plato. He taught that the celibate, ascetic, wise man was the ideal.

Believing bigots

The 'flee the world' stance flooded into Christianity, as monks and nuns were the first-rate Christians, sex was only for procreation and priests slowly were forced to be celibate. If Jesus was the perfect man, then he must have kept all his passions firmly under control, and laughter was frivolity. We should spend more time weeping over our sins, after all! This sick, emaciated excuse for Christianity held tremendous sway, with its exaltation of virginity, hair shirts, and masochistic love of pain for the good of the soul.

> Most people
> carry their religion
> like a headache.
> Spike Milligan

Failure to laugh at ourselves gives us too inflated an ego; a failure to see our own faults makes us demonize others. The laughing, jesting Jesus is a million miles away from the pogroms and inquisitions that have killed Jews and burned heretics over the ages.

Laugh at them, don't burn them!

The church has always had its jokers and fools. Erasmus wrote at the time of the Reformation, when different Christians were fighting and killing each other. He satirized bishops and popes, monks and priests, while remaining a devout believer himself. It was the cant he was after. The Renaissance scholar Michael Screech has said that people like Erasmus were suspect because they did not want to burn anyone! He who knows his own failings cannot condemn another.

Sacred satire

The cutting wit of satire might seem a long way from spirituality, but it can be a very healthy part of it. The best secular satire attacks the proud and the powerful, not letting them conceal their corruptions. As such, it is a social safety valve, and vital to a free society. It is ethical if it does not attack the underdog, the vulnerable, and seeks to pull the carpet out from under the haughty and powerful. And it should be careful with its facts, or it is libellous!

Praise of Folly

The Christian church has had its holy satirical organs down through the ages. Erasmus wrote *Praise of Folly* in 1511, mocking the hypocrisy he saw in the Medieval church. In his introduction he sets out his ethical parameters:

> And to criticize men's lives without mentioning any names – I ask you, does this look like sarcasm, or rather warning and advice? Again, on how many charges am I not my own self-critic? Furthermore, if every type of man is included, it is clear that all vices are censured, not any individual. And so anyone who protests that he is injured betrays his own guilty conscience.

Ship of Fools

The original *Ship of Fools* was a series of 114 woodcuts on a satirical theme, poking fun at the social mores of 1494. The author was Sebastian Brant, but he pulled back from too free a criticism of the church, in fear of his life (this was in the days when everyone expected the Spanish Inquisition!) and he admired Erasmus for his guts. It was popular for generations, and the pictures were reprinted and copied widely.

www.ship-of-fools.com

Today's *Ship of Fools* is a satirical website taking the 'P' out of stuff and nonsense in the contemporary church. For example, 'Gadgets for God' looks at holy tat such as talking tombstones, inflatable Christs and luminous rosary beads. 'Urban Myths' blows apart silly notions in evangelical circles about Proctor and Gamble being run by Satanists. The Mystery Worshipper visits church services and gives an honest and revealing account. The striking thing is the open, free discussion that is encouraged. Many find this refreshing after being in dogmatic churches where they had to follow the party line. It's good to laugh at yourself!

Glad to be in a body

Laughter is so bodily, involving muscles and spasms all over us. It's such a good antidote to the garbage about escaping the body and seeing the material as unspiritual and inferior. It is a part of God's good creation, and the Christian doctrine of the incarnation (when God became man in Jesus) proclaims it as such even louder – God took a body. Laugh along with that one.

God of laughter

God has many names and titles in the Bible. One is 'the God of Abraham, Isaac and Jacob'. 'Isaac' means 'laughter' in Hebrew. God has humour in his name. How sad that religion can be used for repression and fanaticism as well as joy, hope and forgiveness. But *any* ideology can be used or abused – politics is no different. The real problem lies in the darkness of the human heart. Just think how many died or suffered in the gulags of the atheistic Soviet Union.

We can follow the way of Life or Death, and if we are to worship God, let it be a God of Life. Life is for laughing!

Splat!

The crowd hooted and whistled as they raised their custard pies high. Various stewards were distributing these along the rows, using up several cans of foam. Jesus took his final bow and all hell was let loose. Pies flew this way and that, splattering all over him. He couldn't see a thing and slipped on another, hitting the deck with a bang. Jesus was counted down by a referee as all the pies had hit their target. Just before he got to 'ten', up jumped Jesus with a flourish and a fanfare, arms outstretched and a big smile on his face.

'You can't keep this man down!'

Ted and Reg roared until their sides nearly split.

'*He* can come again!'

The last laugh

Any clown worth his salt takes his pratfall and doesn't stay among the custard pies, after all! Jesus was nailed to a cross, but didn't stay dead. Christians say that the resurrection was the biggest joke of all – for he who laughs last, laughs best. If we can believe in the resurrection, then perhaps we can hope that laughter will have the last word in our world.

Putting a Smile on Your Face

Tips to brighten up your day

1. Keep a good joke book/cartoon book by your bed. Go to sleep laughing and wake up laughing.

2. Try to see the ludicrous, funny side of life. Imagine yourself as others see you, and try to laugh at yourself when you are getting worked up.

3. Remember the maxim, 'All work and no play makes Jack a dull boy.' Take time off and don't feel guilty. Relax, unwind, do something you enjoy.

4. Let your hair down from time to time, live a little, let go! There is a clown inside all of us. Is there something you've always wanted to do – hang-glide, bungee jump?

5. Make a list of the ten funniest things that have ever happened to you. Take time out to talk to friends and family about this. You might be surprised what they remember and you can't believe you've forgotten!

6. Organize a comedy party. Have a round-robin joke session; play Twister and other silly games; get people to bring a video of their favourite comedy programme and eat a mound of party food watching them.

Kevin o'Donnell is a former school teacher specialising in Personal and Spiritual Development, and now a practising Anglican priest. Kevin is also a freelance writer who juggles with metaphysics and philosophy, trying to communicate Big Ideas in little words. Speaking metaphorically, our brains are elastic, able to stretch beyond the physical and obvious to be teased by transcendence. If we can't have a laugh, then it's a strange old world, and laughter might be one of the keys to under-standing ourselves. Hence a little book on humour for mind, body and spirit.

Kevin has written educational resources and TV scripts. He is currently the Rector of a busy parish in west Sussex. He is married to Gill, with three lively boys, Maximillian, Oscar, and newly arrived Hector.